AF439744

This gift is for

____

From

____

Moments of Time

Gary Hurst
Mike Kachura
Larry Sides

THOMAS NELSON PUBLISHERS
Nashville

Library of Congress Cataloging-in-Publication Data
See last page

Printed in Singapore
1 2 3 4 5 6 — 98 97 96 95 94 93

Moments of Time

To everything there is a
season,
A time for every purpose under
heaven. . . .
—ECCL. 3:1

God, help me learn to take
life as it comes and enjoy it.

A merry heart does good,
like medicine,
But a broken spirit
dries the bones.
—PROV. 17:22

A merry heart necessitates that we allow ourselves the chance to relax and enjoy the fruits of our labors. Take time to cultivate your sense of humor.

So teach us to number
our days,
That we may gain a heart
of wisdom.
—PS. 90:12

The Africans do not have clocks, but calendars. They count days, not minutes. They live longer, too.

He said, "This is the rest
with which
You may cause the weary
to rest,"
And, "This is the refreshing";
Yet they would not hear.
—ISA. 28:12

Learn to rest when you are weary. And if there is an easier way to do the job, take it.

Be still, and know
that I am God;
I will be exalted
among the nations,
I will be exalted in
the earth!
—PS. 46:10

We perfectionists can revitalize ourselves by being still and knowing that God is God and we are "just" ourselves.

"Who then is greatest in the kingdom of heaven?" . . . "Whoever humbles himself as this little child is the greatest in the kingdom of heaven."
—MATT. 18:1, 4

Christ gives us permission to be little children again. And our heavenly Father promises to meet our needs.

Now the body is . . . for the Lord, and the Lord for the body.
—1 COR. 6:13

Our bodies are the temple of
the Holy Spirit, and God is
concerned about its upkeep.

"It would have been better for us to serve the Egyptians than that we should die in the wilderness."
—EX. 14:12

Like the Israelites, we are sometimes tempted to live in bondage to our work in order to avoid difficulties or gain benefits. Slavery is too high a price for easy living.

"And they brought back word to us, saying, 'It is a good land which the LORD our God is giving us.' Nevertheless you would not go up, but rebelled."
—DEUT. 1:25–26

Risk-taking produces growth. To resist change results in stagnation.

What then shall we say to
these things? If God is for us,
who can be against us?
—ROM. 8:31

We do not need to prove
our strength to anyone. God
is for us.

So He Himself often withdrew into the wilderness and prayed.
—LUKE 5:16

God, help me take the time
to let my body and mind
recuperate from these weeks of
work and to be alone with you.

And He said to them, "Come aside by yourselves to a deserted place and rest a while." For there were many coming and going, and they did not even have time to eat.
—MARK 6:31

Jesus did not model a pattern of burnout. He paced his life. Remember, there is always more to do than you have time to do. You will be stronger if you pace yourself.

There are many plans in a
man's heart,
Nevertheless the LORD's
counsel—that will stand.
—PROV. 19:21

We are often driven by an endless supply of plans. God, help us remember only your purposes will last.

And do not be conformed to
this world, but be transformed
by the renewing of your mind.
—ROM. 12:2

The first step in renewing our minds is to recognize lies we believe about ourselves. The second step is to replace the lies with truth.

Wait on the LORD;
Be of good courage,
And He shall strengthen
your heart;
Wait, I say, on the LORD!
—PS. 27:14

When we try to take control, we lose control. When we relinquish control to God, he gives us the power we desire.

Do not overwork to be rich;
Because of your own
understanding, cease!
—PROV. 23:4

It is often difficult to distinguish between ambition and addiction. God, give us the wisdom to know the difference.

His divine power has given to us all things that pertain to life and godliness, through the knowledge of Him who called us by glory and virtue.
—2 PETER 1:3

If you have a relationship with God, you have already been given everything you need for life and godliness.

"Take heed and beware of covetousness, for one's life does not consist in the abundance of the things he possesses."
—LUKE 12:15

Winning is fun, but not at
the cost of personal integrity.
Our lives can be rich
regardless of what we possess.

"For whoever desires to save
his life will lose it, and
whoever loses his life for My
sake will find it."
—MATT. 16:25

Only when we surrender our lives to Christ will we find the life we are seeking.

"The servant therefore fell down before him, saying, 'Master, have patience with me, and I will pay you all.'"
—MATT. 18:26

Are you trying to repay a debt you cannot repay, or are you waiting for a repayment that can never come?

"He has sent Me . . .
To give them beauty for ashes."
—ISA. 61:1, 3

God is powerful enough to bring good out of the worst of situations.

Two are better than one,
Because they have a good
reward for their labor.
For if they fall, one will lift up
his companion.
But woe to him who is alone
when he falls,
For he has no one to help
him up.
—ECCL. 4:9–10

We all need trusted friends to help us keep our priorities straight.

O LORD, You have searched
me and known me . . .
Such knowledge is too
wonderful for me;
It is high, I cannot attain it.
—PS. 139:1, 6

God already knows you; you cannot surprise him. He responds with mercy and grace.

"And this is eternal life, that they may know You, the only true God, and Jesus Christ whom You have sent."
—JOHN 17:3

Help me, God, to make
eternal life and knowing you,
the only true God and Savior,
my top priority today.

"Come to Me, all you who labor and are heavy laden, and I will give you rest."
—MATT. 11:28

God through Christ can take
every burden we give him.

Who shall separate us from
the love of Christ?
—ROM. 8:35

We often believe that hard work is the only way we can have love. God's love is unconditional.

Not that we are sufficient of ourselves to think of anything as being from ourselves, but our sufficiency is from God.
—2 COR. 3:5

The key to a balanced life is neither to overcompensate for inadequacies nor to deny they exist. This ability rests in our security that God alone is sufficient to provide what we desire.

All things are lawful for me,
but all things are not helpful.
All things are lawful for me,
but I will not be brought under
the power of any.
—1 COR. 6:12

Lord, give me the wisdom to recognize the important things and the strength to resist the rest.

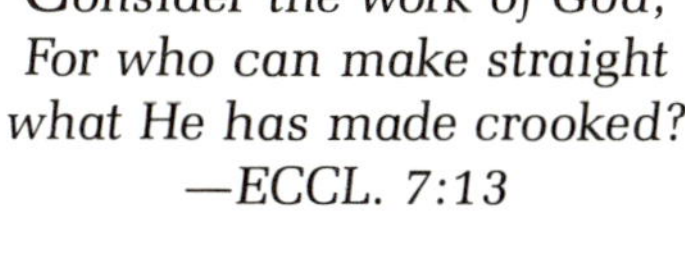

Consider the work of God;
For who can make straight
what He has made crooked?
—ECCL. 7:13

Do not abhor yourself when
you do not see your life
progressing smoothly. God
fully understands your
limitations.

Then He arose and rebuked the wind, and said to the sea, "Peace, be still!" And the wind ceased and there was a great calm.

—MARK 4:39

Just as Jesus is able to speak and command the calmness of the sea, so he is able to command peace in our souls, no matter how turbulent they may seem.

Come and see the works
of God;
He is awesome in His doing
toward the sons of men.
—PS. 66:5

The greatest foe to a balanced life is feeling we have to keep our noses so close to the grindstone that we miss the wonders around us. Plan to spend some time today, slowly enjoying some part of God's creation.

But those who wait on
the LORD
Shall renew their strength;
They shall mount up with
wings like eagles.
—ISA. 40:31

Eagles are able to soar to great heights, not by flapping their wings furiously, but by fully extending them and using the power of the wind. We will soar by using the power of the Lord.

For what will it profit a man if
he gains the whole world, and
loses his own soul?
—MARK 8:36

Don't be held hostage by the words, "If you don't do it, we'll find someone who will."

For we dare not . . . compare ourselves with those who commend themselves. But they, measuring themselves by themselves, and comparing themselves by themselves, are not wise.
—2 COR. 10:12

Perhaps we cannot help the tendency to compare ourselves with others, but we can challenge it when it comes to mind.

[I am] confident of this very thing, that He who has begun a good work in you will complete it until the day of Jesus Christ.

—PHIL. 1:6

God, help me trust that you
will continue to perfect your
work in me.

Be anxious for nothing, but in everything by prayer and supplication, with thanksgiving, let your requests be made known to God.
—PHIL. 4:6

Anxiety flourishes in our lives when we work too much. As we begin trusting God with our work and our lives, our anxiety will decrease.

"The thing that you do is not good. Both you and these people who are with you will surely wear yourselves out. For this thing is too much for you; you are not able to perform it by yourself."
—EX. 18:17–18

Wise leaders delegate
responsibility.

And He is before all things,
and in Him all things consist.
—COL. 1:17

Jesus Christ holds all things together. We don't have to.

*Casting all your care upon
Him, for He cares for you.*
—1 PETER 5:7

Trusting means giving power over to another. God can be trusted with that power. He cares for us.

"In returning and rest you
shall be saved;
In quietness and confidence
shall be your strength."
—ISA. 30:15

God, give us courage to be
still.

*Also it is not good for a soul
to be without knowledge,
And he sins who hastens with
his feet.*
—PROV. 19:2

We are often driven by something that seems to rob us of choices for a balanced lifestyle. To be freed, we must give God control.

"For the heart of this people
has grown dull. . . . Lest they
should understand with their
heart and turn,
So that I should heal them."
—ACTS 28:27

Work can give us a chance to focus on a task while pretending that pain isn't there. But God can handle our pain when we stop to feel it.

Return to your rest,
O my soul.
For the Lord has dealt
bountifully with you.
—PS. 116:7

Never settle critical issues when tired. Get a good night's sleep and approach the issues with a fresh perspective.

" 'You shall love the LORD
your God with all your heart,
with all your soul, and with all
your mind.' This is the first
and great commandment. And
the second is like it: 'You shall
love your neighbor as
yourself.' "
—MATT. 22:37–39

Jesus said that life boils down to three relationships: with God, with other people, and with ourselves. God, help us value these more than work.

Commit your work to the
LORD,
And your thoughts will be
established.
—PROV. 16:3

God, help me learn to take
life as it comes and enjoy it.

**Library of Congress
Cataloging-in-Publication Data**

Hurst, Gary.
　　Moments of time / by Gary Hurst, Mike
　　Kachura, Larry Sides.
　　　　p.　cm.
　　"A Janet Thoma book"
　　ISBN 0-8407-7811-2
　　1. Meditations.　I. Kachura, Mike.
II. Sides, Larry.　III. Title.
BV4832.2.H775　1993
242'.5—dc20　　　　　　　　92-37894
　　　　　　　　　　　　　　　　CIP